DK READERS is a compelling program for beginning readers, designed in conjunction with leading literacy experts, including Dr. Linda Gambrell, Director of the School of Education at Clemson University. Dr. Gambrell has served on the Board of Directors of the International Reading Association and as President of the National Reading Conference.

Beautiful illustrations and superb full-color photographs combine with engaging, easy-to-read stories to offer a fresh approach to each subject in the series. Each DK READER is guaranteed to capture a child's interest while developing his or her reading skills, general knowledge, and love of reading.

The four levels of DK READERS are aimed at different reading abilities, enabling you to choose the books that are exactly right for your child:

Level 1 – Beginning to read
Level 2 – Beginning to read alone
Level 3 – Reading alone
Level 4 – Proficient readers

The "normal" age at which a child begins to read can be anywhere from three to eight years old, so these levels are intended only as a general guideline.

No matter which level you select, you can be sure that you are helping your child learn to read, then read to learn!

DK

LONDON, NEW YORK, MUNICH,
MELBOURNE, and DELHI

Project Editor Mary Atkinson
Art Editor Karen Lieberman
Senior Editor Linda Esposito
Deputy Managing Art Editor
Jane Horne
US Editor Regina Kahney
Production Kate Oliver
Picture Researchers Jo Carlill and
Tom Worsley
Illustrator Pete Roberts

Reading Consultant
Linda B. Gambrell, Ph.D.

First American Edition, 1998
05 06 10 9 8
Published in the United States by DK Publishing, Inc.
375 Hudson Street, New York, New York 10014

Published in Great Britain by Dorling Kindersley Limited.

Library of Congress Cataloging-in-Publication Data
Yorke, Malcolm
    Beastly Tales / by Malcolm Yorke. -- First American ed.
    p.   cm. -- (Dorling Kindersley readers. Level 3)
    Summary: An account of famous monsters including the one
at Loch Ness in Scotland, the Yeti or Abominable Snowman
of the Himalayas, and Bigfoot or Sasquatch of Canada
and the Pacific Northwest.
    ISBN 0-7894-2962-4
    1. Loch Ness monster--Juvenile literature. 2. Yeti--Juvenile
literature. 3. Sasquatch--Juvenile literature. [1. Loch Ness
monster. 2. Yeti. 3. Sasquatch. 4. Monsters.]
I. DK Publishing. Inc. II. Series.
QL89.B44   1998
001.944--dc21   97-38622
                                                        CIP

Color reproduction by Colourscan, Singapore
Printed and bound in China by L Rex Printing Co., Ltd.

The publisher would like to thank the following for their
kind permission to reproduce their photographs:
t=top, b=below, l=left, r=right, c=center
Academy of Applied Science: Robert Rines 15br; **American Museum
of Natural History:** 20tc; **Bruce Coleman:** 37tr, 45tr; **Camera Press:**
Patrick Lichfield 21c; **Fortean Picture Library:** 11c, 31cr; Cliff Crook 3cb,
46c; Rene Dahinden 40tr, 41c, 42cl, 42cr, 43cl, 44cr, 45br, 47tr;
Ivor Newby 17cr; Andrew Trottmann 12tr; Nicholas Witchell 16c;
Mary Evans Picture Library: 5tc, 12br, 13cb, 32tl; **Planet Earth Pictures:**
Anup Shah 4cr; **Rex Features:** 2crb, 6br, 10br, 18cb, 19c, 30c, 33bc, 35c;
Robert Harding Picture Library: 23crb, 23tr; **Royal Geographical Society:**
22bc, 28tr, 28c, 29tc; **Smithsonian Institution:** Museum of the American Indian
40br; **Topham Picturepoint:** 14tc; **Press Association** 30tr.

Jacket: **Fortean Picture Library:** Cliff Crook front bl;
Robert Harding Picture Library: front/background.
All other images © Dorling Kindersley.
For further information see: www.dkimages.com

see our complete product line at

www.dk.com

Contents

READERS

READING
3
ALONE

BEASTLY TALES

YETI, BIGFOOT, AND
THE LOCH NESS MONSTER

Written by Malcolm Yorke

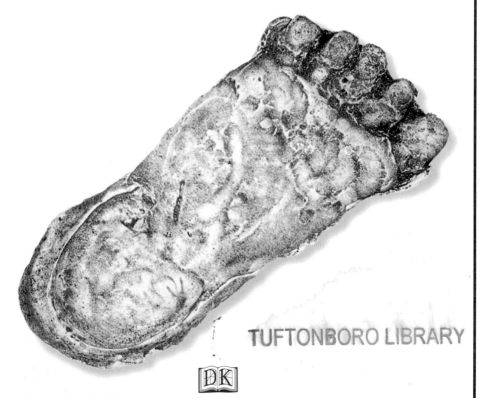

DK

DK Publishing, Inc.

Believe it or not!

All around the world people tell stories about seeing mysterious monsters in remote places. The storytellers are often accused of making things up. But sometimes a discovery is made that proves them right.

Mountain gorillas were discovered by European explorers in 1902.

The Komodo dragon is a meat-eating lizard that can grow bigger than a person, but no one knew about it until 1912.

The Kraken of old Norwegian tales is now believed to be the giant squid, which can grow twice as long as a bus.

Few people believed the stories about a manlike ape in Africa, a dragon in Indonesia, or a huge sea monster with long tentacles. However, we now know these creatures as the mountain gorilla, the Komodo dragon, and the giant squid.

Could there be other large creatures still undiscovered in the world?

The Loch Ness monster

"Dad! Dad! What's that in the loch?" shouted Jim Ayton. It was a calm summer's evening in 1963. Jim was working on his father's farm on Loch Ness, a lake in

Loch Ness lies in northern Scotland.

Scotland, when he looked up to see a strange creature moving silently down the lake. It was huge! Jim had never seen anything like it before.

Loch Ness

Loch Ness is a long, narrow lake surrounded by mountains. It is in a part of Scotland where few people live.

Two men nearby heard Jim's shouts and rushed to join him and his father. The excited group wanted a closer look. They ran to the lake, climbed into a boat, and headed straight toward the creature.

The creature's head looked a bit like a horse's head, only bigger. Its neck stretched nearly 6 feet (2 meters), as tall as a full-grown man. Its snakelike body was as long as a bus. Could it be the legendary Loch Ness monster that people had talked about for years?

Suddenly the creature rose out of
the water. Then it dived. An enormous
wave hit the small boat. It rocked and
swirled around. Had the creature seen
the men? Was it about to attack?

A few seconds later the creature's head reappeared. It was farther away now. The monster seemed more frightened than ferocious! Then it was gone. The men searched and searched for it, but they never saw it again.

It was 20 years before anyone heard the story about what had happened that day. Jim and his father didn't think many people would believe them. But the Aytons and their friends are not the only people who claim to have seen this mysterious monster.

A deep, dark lake

If you were to view the lake, it would be hard to imagine that it has a depth of more than 700 feet (213 meters) – that's deep enough to hide a 42-story building.

This photograph, taken by monster hunter Anthony Shiels 14 years after the Aytons' sighting, seems to show the monster just as the Aytons described it.

One of the earliest known sightings was made more than 1,400 years ago by Saint Columba, a traveling Irish holy man. Legends tell how, in 565 AD, the saint saw a "water monster" attack a swimmer in Loch Ness. When the saint ordered it to leave the swimmer alone, the monster retreated immediately.

Saint Columba is featured on this stained-glass window in a Scottish castle chapel.

Loch legends

There are many legends of water monsters living in other Scottish lakes. The Scottish people call these monsters kelpies.

The Loch Ness monster first became famous in 1933, after a road was built around the steep sides of the Loch Ness valley. Tourists could now explore this remote area for the first time. It was not long before reports of monster sightings began appearing in newspapers all around the world.

The monster is the star attraction on this 1930s' postcard from Loch Ness.

Spotting the monster soon brought rewards. Newspapers would pay a lot of money for a photograph of the monster – even if it was blurred! Fortune seekers, scientists, and monster enthusiasts swarmed around the loch, all wanting to take the best monster picture ever.

Over the years, the searchers used more and more modern equipment. In 1972, an underwater camera produced a close-up of a strange object in the loch. When scientists used a special computer to sharpen up the image, this is what they saw. Could it be one of the monster's flippers?

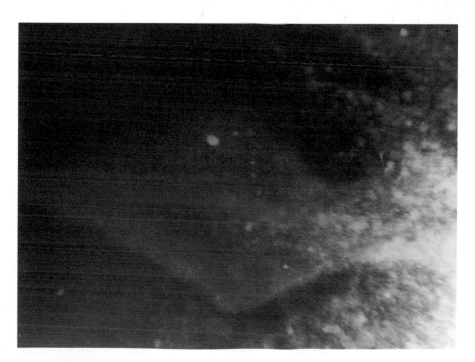

The "flipper" photograph

The underwater photograph seems to show a flipper, but no one can be sure because the image is so grainy. It is hard to see or to take a photograph in the lake water because it is full of tiny pieces of peat, or dead plant material.

In 1987, a team of scientists searched the loch with high-tech equipment for a project called Operation Deepscan. A line of 19 boats, each fitted with a sonar scanner, moved up the loch. What they discovered amazed them.

Sonar scanners

A sonar scanner sends out sound waves. The sound waves bounce back off objects in their way, making a picture of the objects on the sonar screen.

Some scans showed huge objects moving deep in the lake. The objects were bigger than sharks but smaller than whales. Were they huge fish? Or was it a family of Loch Ness monsters? Again the murky water kept the scientists from knowing the answer.

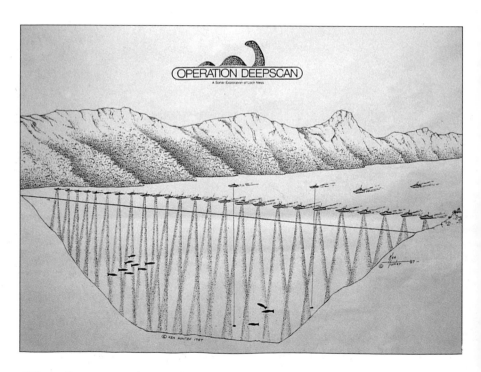

This diagram shows how the boats with sonar scanners moved in a line so that no part of the loch would be missed.

Without clear pictures, scientists must rely on people's descriptions to know what the monster looks like. It seems that the creature has a long, thin neck, a bulky body with four flippers, and a long, powerful tail.

Artists used eyewitness descriptions to design this model of the Loch Ness monster.

No animal living today fits this description. However, one prehistoric creature does.

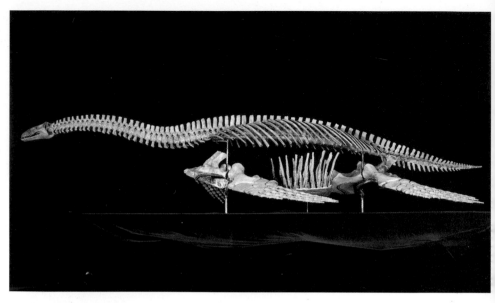

This fossil skeleton of Cryptocleidus is twice as long as an adult person.

Cryptocleidus (krip-toe-KLIE-duss) was a plesiosaur: a huge fish-eating reptile that lived in the sea. Some people think it looked a lot like the Loch Ness monster. However, *Cryptocleidus* is thought to have disappeared from the Earth 70 million years ago! Could it have lived on unnoticed?

Is the Loch Ness monster a survivor from the dinosaur age? Or were the people who saw it simply fooled by boats, logs, shadows, or giant eels? Could some of the sightings be the result of practical jokes? No one knows the truth – yet. ❖

From a distance, it would be easy to mistake this log for a monster. Could everyday things like this explain some of the Loch Ness monster sightings?

Yeti

Even the police felt afraid when they saw the footprints of the beast that attacked Lhakpa Dolma (LAK-pa DOL-ma).

The Himalayan mountains

In 1974, teenager Lhakpa lived in a Nepalese village high in the Himalayan mountains. Each day she climbed partway up Mount Everest to graze a herd of yaks, a type of cattle.

Many Nepalese people live on the slopes of the Himalayas.

The highest in the world
At 29,028 feet (8,848 meters), Mount Everest is the world's highest mountain. It takes weeks to climb to the top.

Lhakpa saw few people on the steep mountain paths. Only Buddhist monks who chose to build their monasteries far from towns and cities lived this high up.

Lhakpa had heard tales of the yeti, an apelike beast said to live in the Himalayas. But the mountains stretched for thousands of miles. She never expected to see one herself.

Like these people, Lhakpa's family were Sherpas – people who first came from eastern Tibet to Nepal around 400 years ago.

One day, as Lhakpa grazed the herd, she noticed that the yaks seemed restless. She thought that a bear or a snow leopard might be nearby. Lhakpa led the yaks to a clear, snow-fed stream. She drank herself, then watched as the yaks fed on the tough mountain grasses.

Suddenly Lhakpa heard a strange, deep grunt. She whirled around as a huge, two-legged creature came rushing toward her. It was a yeti! Terrified, she broke into a run. But it was too late.

The yeti grabbed Lhakpa in its long, hairy arms. She screamed and kicked, but the yeti was too strong.

Then, without warning, the beast dropped her into the icy stream and turned on her yaks. With powerful blows, it quickly killed three of the enormous beasts. Lhakpa crawled out of the stream and ran home as fast as she could. When the police investigated the scene, they found the yeti's large footprints – but not the yeti.

Lhakpa's story is similar to many other tales of the yeti reported by people living in the Himalayas.

Mountaineers, drawn by the challenge of exploring the world's highest mountain range, have also told chilling tales of this apelike beast.

In 1951, mountaineer Eric Shipton and his party were exploring an unknown part of the Himalayas when they came across a line of strange footprints in the snow.

Eric Shipton

Michael Ward, one of Eric Shipton's climbing companions, compares his own footprints, on the right, with those of the creature.

Eric Shipton placed his 13-inch (33-centimeter) ice ax in this photograph to show the size of the footprint.

The footprints looked similar to human footprints – but they were twice as wide. They had sunk much deeper into the snow than the climbers' boot prints so they must have been made by an incredibly heavy creature. Most amazing of all, the clear toe prints showed that the creature was walking barefoot in the freezing snow!

In 1970, another mountaineer had an even closer encounter with a yeti. Don Whillans was climbing in the Himalayas when a Sherpa guide called out, "Yeti coming!"

Don Whillans

The yeti seems skilled at surviving on its own in a frozen environment (photograph shows model).

Don looked up, but only caught a quick look at the black, apelike figure before it disappeared behind a ridge.

The next day Don found the creature's footprints in the snow. They were about the same size as his boot prints. The Sherpa guide told him that the prints were made by a baby yeti.

A drawing of a yeti based on eyewitness descriptions

A yeti illustration from a French magazine

Later that night Don saw the creature again. He was looking out of his tent into bright moonlight when it came loping along. It headed for a clump of trees and began pulling the branches.

Don grabbed his binoculars. But the creature suddenly noticed him and ran across the mountain and out of sight.

The number of yeti sightings caught the interest of some scientists. They studied photos and plaster casts of yeti footprints, then compared them with other animal footprints. They decided that the yeti prints could not have been made by a bear, an ape, an antelope, or any other known animal.

Aside from footprints, little evidence for the yeti has been found. There was excitement when a Nepalese monk gave a yeti scalp to Sir Edmund Hillary, one of the first men to climb Mount Everest.

The yeti scalp given to Sir Edmund Hillary

Edmund Hillary handed the scalp over to scientists. It turned out to be a fake made of goat-antelope hair.

But yeti footprints are still being found. In 1992, Julian Freeman-Atwood found footprints on a glacier that no one had climbed for 30 years.

Monster mania
Fascination with the yeti has inspired many stories. Some are serious news articles, others are just good fun.

Will the mystery of the yeti ever be solved? What sort of creature is it? Where does it sleep? How does it find enough food on the snow-covered mountains? Maybe you will be the one who discovers the answers! ❖

Yeti footprints have been discovered on other mountains in Asia, as well as the Himalayas. These footprints found by Julian Freeman-Atwood were on a glacier in Mongolia.

Bigfoot

Albert Ostman was expecting a quiet time when he headed into a forest near Vancouver, Canada, for a camping trip in 1924.

The mysterious bigfoot is said to live in forests in the Pacific Northwest.

One night, though, he noticed that something had been searching through his pack. He thought it was a porcupine or a bear. But it turned out to be neither.

In the middle of the night, Albert woke with a jolt. Someone or something was lifting him up inside his sleeping bag! Albert was trapped. For hours, he was bumped and bounced around as something carried him over rough ground.

When daylight came, Albert got a look at his captor – and it wasn't alone!

Four huge, hairy beasts – three
adults and a child – surrounded him.
They looked half ape and half human.
To Albert's relief, they did not hurt him,
but they would not let him leave.

For six days he was their prisoner. Then one day the oldest male ate some tobacco from Albert's pack and soon became ill. As he rolled on the ground in pain, Albert made his escape.

Back in Vancouver, locals told Albert that his captors were bigfeet.

These mysterious creatures have been sighted thousands of times in the forests of the Pacific Northwest.

Albert Ostman photographed 33 years after his capture

A bigfoot is said to look similar to a yeti, although it could be even bigger. Some people have reported seeing bigfeet that were 8 feet (2.5 meters) tall. The creatures are covered in hair, and have flat faces, short necks, and wide shoulders.

Bigfoot's many names
Native Americans have told stories of bigfeet for centuries. Different tribes give the creature different names, such as Sasquatch or Oh-mah-ah.

Comparing a possible bigfoot footprint (left) with an adult man's foot (right) shows how the creature got its name.

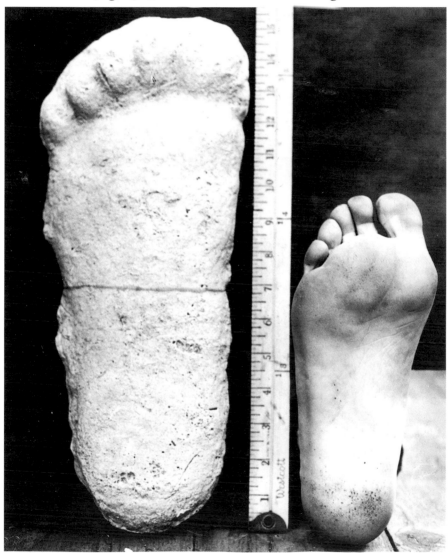

A bigfoot has never been caught, dead or alive, but in 1967, two California men claimed that they captured one on film.

According to Roger Patterson, he and a friend set off on horseback to find a bigfoot. Armed with a movie camera, they went searching in an area where there had already been some sightings.

These four photographs are from the actual film shot by Roger Patterson.

They were riding alongside a stream when they rounded a corner and saw a bigfoot by the water's edge. Roger's horse reared up, throwing Roger to the ground. He jumped up and began filming.

The bigfoot ran toward the forest. Roger ran after it, filming the whole time. Some scientists thought the film was a fake, but they couldn't prove it.

Experts in the US and Russia studied the way the bigfoot moved. They decided that it would be very difficult for anyone in a fur suit to run in such a natural way.

Roger had made plaster casts of the bigfoot's footprints. The casts showed that the creature's feet were 14½ inches (37 centimeters) long. Each foot had five toes, like a human foot, but the sole of the foot was much flatter.

Roger Patterson holding the plaster casts of the bigfoot's footprints

Bigfoot food

Judging from eyewitness stories, it seems that bigfeet eat mainly plants, but they have also been spotted eating fish and small animals, such as marmots.

marmot

The same year, logger Glen Thomas claims he saw three bigfeet farther north in Oregon State. The largest one was moving a pile of huge rocks. Finally it reached a nest of marmots. From behind the trees, Glen watched the bigfoot eat the animals one by one.

Later, investigators found that the rocks had been moved recently and that marmots did nest in that area.

Glen Thomas on the rocks where he saw the bigfeet

Since then, more and more people have produced evidence of bigfeet. In 1995, a forest patrol officer in Washington State claimed that he heard splashes and turned around to see a bigfoot looking straight at him.

One of the photographs taken by a forest patrol officer in 1995

Luckily he had a camera with him and was able to take clear photographs. Experts argue about whether or not the photographs are real.

No one has collected absolute proof that bigfeet exist, but the evidence seems overwhelming. Tape recordings show they grunt, whistle, roar, bark, and howl. Thousands of footprints have been found in mud, sand, and snow.

What should we do next? Some people think we should trap or shoot one. Others say we should leave them alone.

What do you think? ❖

Glossary

Abominable snowman
Another name for the yeti (see Yeti).

Bigfoot
A large, hairy, apelike beast that some people believe lives in Pacific Northwestern forests.

Cryptocleidus
A plesiosaur that lived in the sea around Scotland 70 million years ago (see Plesiosaur).

Evidence
Anything that people can show to prove that they are telling the truth, such as photographs.

Eyewitness
A person who says he or she has seen (witnessed) a particular event.

Glacier
A huge mass of ice that slides downhill very slowly, often carving out a valley as it moves.

Himalayas
The world's highest mountain range. It runs through Nepal, Tibet, India, and other countries.

Kelpie
A water monster with a horse-shaped head that some people believe lives in Scottish rivers and lakes.

Kraken
A sea monster from Norwegian myths, now believed to be the giant squid.

Loch
A Scottish lake.

Loch Ness monster
A large monster that some people believe lives in Loch Ness, Scotland.

Mountaineer
A person who climbs mountains.

Plaster cast
A model made by pouring plaster into a shape and letting it harden.

Plesiosaur
A large swimming reptile with a long neck and four flippers that swam in the sea millions of years ago (see *Cryptocleidus*).

Prehistoric
Anything from before written human history.

Sasquatch
A name for bigfoot that comes from a Native American (Salish) word meaning hairy man (see Bigfoot).

Sherpas
People originally from eastern Tibet now living in Nepal.

Sonar scanner
A machine that sends out sound waves and analyzes their echoes to build up a picture of an object.

Yak
A type of cattle with long, thick hair kept by people living in the Himalayas.

Yeti
A hairy, apelike beast that many people believe lives in the Himalayas and the mountains of Mongolia.